Charity Dye

The Story-Teller's Art

A Guide to the Elementary Study of Fiction, Intended for High Schools....

Charity Dye

The Story-Teller's Art
A Guide to the Elementary Study of Fiction, Intended for High Schools....

ISBN/EAN: 9783337158712

Printed in Europe, USA, Canada, Australia, Japan

Cover: Foto ©Paul-Georg Meister /pixelio.de

More available books at **www.hansebooks.com**

THE

STORY-TELLER'S ART

A GUIDE TO THE
ELEMENTARY STUDY OF FICTION

INTENDED FOR HIGH SCHOOLS AND ACADEMIES

BY

CHARITY DYE

TEACHER OF ENGLISH, INDIANAPOLIS HIGH SCHOOL

" But art, — wherein man nowise speaks to men,
Only to mankind, — art may tell a truth
Obliquely, do the thing shall breed the thought,
Nor wrong the thought, missing the mediate word,
. . . .
So write a book shall mean beyond the facts,
Suffice the eye and save the soul beside."
— ROBERT BROWNING.

BOSTON, U.S.A.
GINN & COMPANY, PUBLISHERS
The Athenæum Press
1899

PREFACE.

THESE pages have grown out of class room experience. They are based upon the assumption that fiction not only fills a needed place in the curriculum of the secondary school, but that it furnishes a means for language discipline and the acquisition of knowledge; that it develops the power to appreciate and to express, and gives to the student a fullness of life that cannot be supplied in any other way. It also introduces him to the world of institutions and thus enables him to take part in the affairs of life.

That the study of fiction is not beyond the grasp of secondary pupils is proved by the exercises given from the papers of the students themselves.

No attempt has been made herein to distinguish closely between the short story and the novel; both are handled in a general way. One merit claimed for the book is its general character. Secondary pupils should view the subject as a whole first.

I am indebted to Dr. Oscar L. Triggs, of the University of Chicago, for criticism and assistance in proof reading, and to Mrs. Lois G. Hufford, of the Indianapolis High School, for helpful suggestions.

1897.   CHARITY DYE.

CONTENTS.

———◦⊶◦———

THE STORY-TELLER'S ART.

I. TO THE TEACHER.

In determining the place and time for the study of fiction in the curriculum of the secondary school, the place of the story in the whole educational system commands attention ; and what applies to the use of the story throughout applies in a much larger way to the serious study of fiction in the secondary school. How can the story be made a more potent factor in education ? How shall it be used ? What shall be the basis for the selection of stories for use ? Must utility be always in view ? Shall a story never be selected in and for itself independent of a lesson in ethics, geography, history, science, or composition ? Must a reading of " Tom, the Water Baby," be followed by a discourse upon cleanliness, or left to teach its own lesson ? When the aesthetic features of a story bring response from a student and when the content enkindles his soul, is not the use of the story for its own sake justified, even though it illustrate no single point in the curriculum? These are serious questions and ought to be seriously met in the consideration of the story as an educative factor.

The nature of the story should determine whether it be used independently or in connection with other subjects. While one story must be given by itself as a work of art, another may best be used in correlation with the subject which it illustrates. Story has always formed the borderland to the study of the world of nature and the world of institutions. What better introduction to the study of history than story? It gives the thread of fact in its setting as in life ; it gives it in its atmosphere, in its perspective, in its picturesqueness. How much more is added to a child's knowledge of the bravery of the Puritan heart if, instead of hearing in plain language that not one went back on the " Mayflower," he is told this in the story form, and is thereby made to enter into the feelings of the lonely Priscilla watching from the shore the receding sail of the " Mayflower " as it goes without her to all that she loves and holds dear.

Cooper, Helen Hunt, and Longfellow have made the Indian a reality. The story of Washington's trip to Governor Dinwiddie, his winter at Valley Forge, and selections from Lowell's Washington Elm show us the most august figure in American history. The simple story of Lincoln's life, "Uncle Tom's Cabin," and stories from Whittier's war poems fix the meaning of the triumph of freedom. Then for the distinctive local features of the various sections: New England can be found for the young in "Stories from Grandfather's Chair" by Hawthorne and in Mary E. Wilkins's stories. Thomas Nelson Page has shown the Old Dominion; Mrs. McEnery Stuart, the lower South; Bret Harte, the Pacific slope; Hamlin Garland and Octave Thanet, the central West; Charles Egbert Craddock, Tennessee; James Lane Allen, Kentucky; Cable, the Gulf region; Davis, New York; and Riley, Indiana.

The stories of Horatius at the bridge, Marcus Curtius jumping into the gulf of the Forum, Regulus who, after advising the Romans never to make peace with Carthage, went back to chains and death, Fabricius who could not be frightened by elephants upon one day nor bribed by gold on the next, and Cincinnatus who could leave the plow to rule the state and return to the plow, contain the genius of Roman history.

The stories that cluster around Marathon
introduce one to the true spirit of Greek civili-
zation; they show the struggle between the
ancient and the modern world.   There is the
story of the mound over the ninety-two Athe-
nians who fell in the battle; the picture of the
power of Asia that had never been conquered;
the culture of Athens; the terror of the battle
itself and of the part taken in it not only by
the soldiers of Greece but by the gods and early
heroes and strange personages.   Browning tells
of Echetlos, the wielder of the plowshare, and
Pheidippides, the runner who ran all the way
to Sparta for aid.   The poet Aeschylus fought
in this battle.   With Aeschylus can come in his
tragedies of Prometheus and Agamemnon, which
take one into the heart of Grecian mythology.
The Oedipus and Antigone of Sophocles now
belong in order and it is in place to tell how
Sparta redeemed herself at Thermopylae and to
make familiar the inscription at the Pass of
Thermopylae :

> Go, tell the Spartans, thou that passest by,
> That here obedient to their laws we lie.

And so from this center of victory the ancient
world can be made real through ancient story.

It is unnecessary to note at length how the

Norse mythology contains the seriousness of that nation. The story of Odin's giving his right eye for wisdom, of Thor's exploits, and of Balder the beautiful enlist the student's admiration for a people who could look upon icebergs and form a theology. Nor is there time to praise that admirable book, "Ten Boys on the Road from Long Ago to Now." That alone would interpret the expressions "historic view" and "historic evolution."

To come nearer home, in "The Talisman" and in "Ivanhoe" one has chivalry made real to him; he sees its spirit and learns its practices. He watches the knights as they ride into the lists and engages in their combats. He sees the chivalry of the bold outlaw Robin Hood and also feels the spirit of chivalry as practiced by the heathen Saladin, who far excels the leader of the Christian host, Richard of the Lion Heart. One is moreover taken into the Crusades and touches Palestine here as he touched Persia in connection with Greece. He also sees how the Jews were persecuted in England; and the sight of King John brings up the Magna Charta and the valley of Runnymede. Here he also sees the conquered Saxon and the Norman conqueror and learns of the gradual change in speech that went on after the conquest.

Story can do much toward making plain to the child the use of the earth as his home in the midst of physical forces and life. "Seaside and Wayside" and the various "Nature Readers" have shown this. "Seven Little Sisters" is unparalleled as a study of the earth as a home.

In Robert Browning's poem "Development" he tells how he was beguiled by degrees into the full-fledged Greek scholar. First he played Troy, then heard the myths told, then he read the translations, then studied the original, and, lastly, he translated Greek literature into English.

Having decided upon the use of the story, what method of presentation shall be used? The analyzer, on one side, would have it studied; would have every figure in it walk on four feet; every motive in it traced out; every character in it measured by a tape-line; every description in it located and tested as to its accuracy. \The over-sensitive critic in aesthetics, on the other hand, exclaims in horror: "Art is not capable of analysis; it is to be felt: it is to teach by unconscious influence. We resent definition, explanation. We wish to be left to our own impressions. The child's imaginative mind clings to its images and does not wish them rendered into prose reality. A child resents your showing that its doll Cinderella is sawdust and muslin."

Now, neither extreme seems adequate to the right presentation of literary art. Since great art appeals to the whole being, it is clear that the part of a story that appeals to the intellect is capable of analysis, and that in all stories there are parts which may be explained; it is also clear that what appeals directly to the emotions must be left to the unsounded sea of feeling. It seems safest and most in keeping with the treatment of literature as art to omit the analysis if one cannot decide just what and how much to explain.

There are some things that have been settled. One is that it is far better for students to become thoroughly acquainted with a few of the best stories than it is for them to have a superficial knowledge of a greater number. Another thing is that a sympathetic, intelligent reading of a story is one of the best ways of interpreting it. To read a story well requires a pleasant voice (if read orally), the power to appreciate the point, understand the characters, feel the humor and the pathos, and enjoy the descriptions. A story should be well told as well as well read. Indeed, it is doubtful whether one really enjoys a story to its full extent until he can tell it. It is a very significant fact that little children love the same story repeated.

Familiarity with a few of the best stories being secured, one can begin instruction by incidental comment at first and continue to call attention to what is the most essential that all should know until a critical study is reached. This ought not to be below the high school, where the story can be studied as art in connection with other phases of English.

A modern writer says : "There are times in a child's life when it suddenly leaps into larger growth, as the imprisoned bud blooms larger than its promise. . . . Knowledge comes to the child, especially all the subtler knowledge of time, of space, of love, in a vague, indefinite, unconscious way, developing out of the child's organic self as a flower blooms. This knowledge comes to definite knowledge for an instant only and then returns to the sub-consciousness, waiting the next day of warm sun, shining water, and smell of spring. Each time it stays longer, till at last the child can contemplate his own thought and finally express it. These times form our real life epochs." [1]

---

[1] Hamlin Garland in " Rose of Dutcher's Coolly."

Familiarity with all of the best things not only assumes the value of impressions, but gives definiteness to impressions. It provides for comparisons ; it makes associations. Those who know Hawthorne's " Great Stone Face " remember that familiarity with it was what made it the great transforming power in Ernest ; that it was first to him only a face on the mountain side ; then as the years passed it suggested to him the benignity that must be in a spirit to express such majestic calm as he saw there ; this benignity and calm through contemplation entered into his life as a motive : and the result is known, — the poet, the man of insight, came and pronounced the likeness.

Familiarity with the poet's thought in the poet's phrase is essential. When the story comes in the form of some of the great heroic ballads the language of poetry is read as a foreign tongue by resolving it into prose. Poetry should be appreciated through its own language and not through that language made into prose. In the ballad there is a double artistic form, — the story proper and the poet's thought in the poet's phrase. " The true aim of culture," says Mr. Corson, " is to induce soul states or conditions, soul attitudes. . . . Literary knowledge and literary culture are two quite distinct things

— so distinct that a student may possess a large fund of one and be almost destitute of the other."

When Tennyson's " May Queen " or " Enoch Arden " is done over into prose the very things that made Tennyson the master of his time, — his music and his exquisite phrase, — are destroyed. That vivid imagery in which " Enoch Arden " abounds and the rhythmic swell to which the spirit keeps time are lost.

To advocate the use of stories in and for themselves is to imply that such stories exist. Indeed, one suffers from the poverty of riches ; one does not enjoy what he has. Many are still satisfied with the old and agree with Julian Hawthorne in giving Hans Christian Andersen a high place. Some persons still interpret life by " The Ugly Duckling," " The Bottle Neck," " The Five Peas in One Pod," " The Flax," and others of Andersen's stories, which have a subtle, an indefinable charm in them. For pure imagination the " Arabian Nights " are still good, even if they are pronounced inartistic. Dickens's " Child's Dream of a Star," Charles Lamb's " Dream Children," " The Dog of Flanders," Warner's " Hunting of the Deer " are good stories. Poe's " Gold Bug " shows great power of intellect. Hawthorne's stories, all of them, exercise a weird charm over the reader. Homer makes the rising generation, as he made Hugo, twenty feet taller to read him. Sarah Orne Jewett's " White Heron" is a sweet story. Curtis's " Prue and I" is unsurpassed in its idyllic quality. Kipling's " Brushwood Boy" is an artistic short story. The selection of stories is largely an individual matter. A fond grandmother said the other day that her little granddaughter liked " Barnaby Rudge" better than any other book. It was guessed why, when she told that the child had heard the mother read it to the father. The mother's sympathetic voice and the child's desire to share the enjoyment of her elders were in favor of her liking the book. One must discover the best for himself. One can do this by trying stories first upon himself and testing them by his own innate sense of fitness. This having been done, he can try them on his pupils. The best story sometimes fails to fit. If this happens to be the case, the teacher can tell it as best he can, giving only essentials. Sometimes it is best to lay a story aside till it is called for. Common sense always comes to one's aid.

" The Place of the Story in Early Education," by Sarah E. Wiltse, is interesting. She shows

how a kindergartner uses and believes in the
power of the story to mold character.   She
would not tell a story without in some way
connecting it with the deed or tendency she
wished to correct.   As a companion to this
book, Julian Hawthorne in his chapter "Literature for Children" brings up the other side,
and expresses himself concerning the moral
wrong done to children by Miss Edgeworth's
"Frank" and "Parents' Assistant."   He feels
this especially with regard to himself.   He
believes that one ought not to talk down to
children, for they are most formidable literary
critics.   Horace E. Scudder has given good
advice upon this subject.

Mr. Robert Collyer has told of the value of
a story chosen in and for itself.   He says : "Do
you want to know how I manage to talk to you
in this simple Saxon?   I will tell you.   I read
Bunyan, Crusoe, and Goldsmith when I was a
boy, morning, noon, and night.   All the rest
was task work.   These were my delight, with
the stories in the Bible and in Shakespeare,
when at last the mighty master came within
our doors. . . . I took to these as I took to
milk, and, without the least idea what I was
doing, got the taste for simple words into the
very fiber of my nature. . . . I could not go

home for Christmas, 1839, and was feeling sad
about it all, for I was only a boy ; and, sitting
by the fire, an old farmer came in and said : ·I
notice thou 'rt fond of reading, so I brought thee
summat to read.' It was Irving's ·Sketch
Book.' I had never heard of it. I went at it
and was as · them that dream.' No such delight
had touched me since the old days of Crusoe.
I saw the Hudson and the Catskills, took poor
Rip at once into my heart, as everybody does,
pitied Ichabod while I laughed at him, thought
the old Dutch feast a most admirable thing,
and long before I was through all regret at my
lost Christmas had gone down the wind, and I
had found out there are books and books. That
vast hunger never left me. . . . Now, give a
boy a passion like this for anything, books or
business, painting or farming, mechanism or
music, and you give him thereby a lever to lift
his world and a patent of nobility if the thing
he does is noble."

When it is believed that a classic story
classic in that it conforms to the highest art
standards — has a place in education in and for
itself, whether it illustrates a particular thing
or nothing ; when it is believed that a story
answers its end if it in some way appeals to the
imagination, develops the aesthetic emotions,

elevates the nature, kindles the soul, or increases the sympathy, and adds to fullness of life, — when this is believed, the appreciative power will be so quickened that the fitting selection will be detected by an almost unconscious process. Coarseness in language or in tone will at once offend. The subtle undertow in a story will be appreciated. There will then be placed before the youth only that which makes for right-mindedness, that which is wholesome, sweet, that which has the sunshine in it. The story as an educative means is life in miniature, and what is fitter to sustain life than life itself?

Emerson well sets forth the aim in the study of fiction; it is to give the student the power to read the "poetry of affairs, to fuse the circumstances of to-day; not to use Scott's antique superstitions or Shakespeare's, but to convert those of the nineteenth century and of the existing nations into universal symbols. . . . 'Tis easy to repaint the mythology of the Greeks, the feudal castle, the crusade, the martyrdoms of mediaeval Europe : but to point out where the same creative force is now working in our own houses and public assemblies, to convert the vivid energies acting at this hour, in New York and Chicago and San Francisco, into universal symbols requires a sublime and commanding thought. . . . The test is to take the passing day with its news, its cares, its fears, and to hold it up to divine reason till it is seen to have a purpose and beauty and to be related to the eternal order of the world." Certainly not the least among the means employed to reach this noble end is the story-teller's art.

II. TO THE STUDENT.

You have come to the study of fiction, but fiction is not new to you. You have long known of fairies and felt the charm of that magic phrase "Once upon a time." You know Moses and David and Joseph in the Bible; you have joined Hercules in his labors; have helped Siegfried fight the dragon; been with Ulysses in his wanderings; lived on the island with Crusoe; stood at the bridge with Horatius and at Thermopylae with Leonidas; and have gone forth on chivalric errands with King Arthur and his knights. Indeed, you have done enough to be ready to learn of the story-teller and to study his art seriously.

The Story-teller. While the story-teller has always been upon the road of time and his object has always been the same, — to give pleasure and cheer the way, — yet he started out with a very simple beginning. At first, perhaps, he only sang at the feasts and told of the wondrous deeds of gods and heroes, or of the love between fair lady and gentle knight. As the journey lengthened the story-teller's province was enlarged ; he warned as well as amused, and gave us the allegory. Now he would analyze sentiment, indulging in the wildest fancy. Again he would confine himself to an account of the barest facts of the commonplace. By and by he translated tales from other nations. Pride in his art grew with his experience ; he learned from the enlarged life around him ; he used better language, had wider views, more confidence in himself, and began to write upon his own surroundings and thoughts and feelings.

There came a time when he almost stopped story-telling to listen to the players of the great Elizabethan dramas. He learned from his listening. The players had their day and the story-teller began again with renewed vigor, now to be called the novelist, and to have every province of life open for the supply of his materials and to have his writings classed among the arts.

Fiction as Art. — As art, fiction appeals to the mind, just as painting, sculpture, architecture.

and other art forms appeal to it. By degrees you will find rhythm in the rise and fall, the climaxes and sub-climaxes, the critical and commonplace moments of a novel. You will appreciate balance and proportion in its parts and in its progress to turning point and from there to close. You will have intellectual satisfaction in its plot or design applied to life and will note how motive determines deed and how the deed can be traced back to the motive from which it sprang. You will see local coloring in the harmonious pictures of life and its environment. You will appreciate the shade and perspective in the delicate, gradual leadings to and from the critical moments, till each event is seen to grow out of the preceding one, and that which happens seems to be the only thing which could happen under the circumstances.

Scope of the Novel. — The novel is to-day the medium through which mind speaks to minds upon matters ranging from the greatest to the least moment. It is the medium through which the artistic literary sense delights most to express itself. To such an extent is this true that the players are no longer in the front. They are seeing their art applied by the story-teller.

The future of the novel no one can tell : but
all may be sure that its expression of life must
be adequate to life, or it will, in the nature of
things, have to draw a halt. Nature avenges
any lopping off of one side of life here as she
does elsewhere ; her laws are inexorable. This
much seems true at least : Art cannot be sus-
tained when it is based upon the assumption
that environment, heredity, and habit are all the
factors needed in making up the final result ;
there is a fourth factor, — spirit, — which cannot
be counted out nor counted in, in any definite
certainty of measure, but it *must* be counted in
if the story-teller's art is to hold in the future
the place it holds to-day as a great shaping
factor in the life of our time. Charles Reade
says :

" I have labored to make my readers realize
those appalling facts of the day which most
men know but not one in a thousand compre-
hends and not one in a hundred thousand realizes, until fiction — which, whatever you may
have been told to the contrary, is the highest,
widest, noblest, and greatest of all the arts —
comes to his aid, studies, penetrates, digests the
hard facts of chronicles and blue books and
makes the dry bones live." — *Critic*, November
19, 1896.

The Short Story. — The latest development in the story-teller's art is the artistic short story. It was one of our own countrymen, Edgar Allan Poe, who founded the school of the artistic short story. The French were the first to discover this and to apply Poe's rules as laid down in his essay, " The Philosophy of Composition." Poe advanced the idea of commencing at climax and working forward to beginning, and also that of first studying motives and then constructing character therefrom. Upon this theory is based the whole " Sherlock Holmes " family of stories. The artistic short story is modeled upon the pattern of the drama and has marked characteristics. Fiction is here seen for the first time as a balanced whole. It is prophesied that this form will affect the future novel, both as to structure and length. The art in the pattern short story may be realized by comparing the stories of Maupassant with the " Arabian Nights," which live because of their appeal to the imagination and not because of their artistic structure. They lack perspective and their quick succession of events shows no proportion. They do not conceal the knowledge and skill which the modern artist conceals in his work.

In the *McClure's Magazine* for November, 1896, Mrs. Elizabeth Phelps Ward says that the short story is imperfectly understood as a form of fiction; that, while it is already a highly developed specimen of workmanship, it is destined to become far more exquisite than it now is. She thinks a short magazine story one of the finest forms of expression. No inspiration is too noble for it ; no amount of work too severe for it.

Writers of Short Stories. — Kipling is at present the prince of short-story writers in England (though his home is in America). The artistic short stories of character-study rank high. Henry James leads in the study of character. Mary E. Wilkins is pronounced by critics as the most artistic of women writers in this field, and, though narrow in range, she excels in effective dramatic structure, in selecting significant detail, and in good judgment. " The New England Nun " conforms to all the requirements of the artistic short story. Tolstoi holds an undisputed place as a writer of the short story, and the praise accorded to his " Master and Man " is well deserved. His stories " The Long Exile " and " Does a Man Need Much Land ? " are as good.

This glance at the story-teller and his art shows that to study fiction is to study life ; it is to know character and all that goes to the making of character. It is to increase the love of literary art and to see its relation to the other fine arts.

III. MATERIALS.

No artist creates the materials out of which he forms his art-product. George Eliot embodied much of her own experience in "Mill on the Floss." Shakespeare found in legend and in history the substance that was ready to shape itself into ever-living dramas at the touch of his genius. Wagner harmonized the folk-songs of Germany in his "Meistersinger," and Raphael painted the Sistine Madonna in the flowering of an art period which had for its inheritance all that had been done since Cimabue, over two hundred years before, carried his crude picture of Mother and Child in procession before an adoring multitude.

Sources of Materials. — The sources from which the story-teller gets the materials for his art are the world of nature and the world of man.

Materials from Nature. — The world of nature furnishes him natural scenery, animal and plant life ; the movements and forces of nature and the various natural phenomena seen in the roll of the seasons, the courses of day and night, in storm and calm, in the stars set in blue, in the music of the pines, and in all the subtle influences that appeal to the spirit of man. He uses the materials gathered from the external world to give a setting or background to his story, to give it coloring, or to reflect the mood of the story. He may also use it for purely artistic purposes, *i.e.*, to increase the sense of the sublime or the sense of reverence, to furnish contrast, to foreshadow coming events, or to relieve tension.

Materials from the World of Man. — The world of man furnishes the story-teller with materials from human life lived individually and under the institutions of government, church, industry, education, and the other social institutions that foster progress in social life. This realm gives him superstition, legend, history, travel, literature, science, and art, and brings him into touch with other times and places. In addition to these things the world of man furnishes language or the means by which the story-teller communicates his thought. Since he concerns himself mainly in depicting life, he makes most use of the elements that go to the making of character. He employs all the thoughts, passions, loves, hates, ambitions,

the depths of sorrow or the heights of happiness
to portray his characters in living relations.
He puts these attributes into human actions
from which are to be learned their " unsermonized " lessons. Some novelists take a single
attribute and study it in all varieties of its
manifestation before proceeding to embody it in
character ; others prefer to let real life set forth
its imperfect portrayal of attributes ; and so the
way in which materials are used determines to
a great extent the species to which a work of
fiction belongs.

The Story-Teller's own Power. — Within himself the story-teller finds his imagination the
great creative power without which he could
not form his crude materials, gathered here
and there, into artistic wholes. It is the imagination that develops plot, furnishes situations, shapes character, and uses nature to
create a life that is often more vivid than the
one actually lived by the reader. The story-
teller furthermore assumes that an appreciative
response will follow the appeal made by his
work, that what has come from mind will attract
mind. Shakespeare doubtless never forgot
that he was a playwright and that he must
appeal to people.

Suggestive Questions.

1. Can an author create his materials?
2. What are the sources from which he gets them?
3. Give examples of the use made of materials by great authors, artists, and musical composers.
4. What faculty of mind is it that constructs the art product out of the raw materials from the world of man and the world of nature?
5. Classify materials used in stories which you know, as follows : —

    I. Materials from the external world.

        1) Scenes — the nature of — distinctive feature of.
        2) Sounds in nature — from what source — the sea — the wind — other movements of nature — animals.
        3) The movements and forces of nature. Locate and describe them.
        4) How does the author use nature in this story?
        5) From which source does the author draw most material?

6) Has he used nature as a setting or as an aid in developing his characters?

II. From the world of humanity.

1) What people are portrayed?

2) What attributes of man are brought prominently forth? *I.e.*, love, hate, jealousy, courage, ambition, selfishness, or any passion.

3) What material is used from institutional life?

4) Is the love pictured that (*a*) between maiden and lover? (*b*) parent and child? (*c*) friend and friend? (*d*) ruler and subject?

5) Has the author used history — tradition — superstition? In what way?

6) What tradition used by Hawthorne in "The Great Stone Face"? What historical custom used by Scott in "The Lady of the Lake"? What legend used by Irving in "Sleepy Hollow"?

7) Note the harmony between the storm and the progress of the story in "David Copperfield." What does it show?

IV.   THE SETTING.

The setting, or the time, place, and surroundings in which the scenes of the story are laid, forms an important part of fiction.   Unless the characters and events are put in the time and place in which they belong, the story loses force.   Many writers so closely identify their characters with their setting that they are called "novelists of the soil."   Mary E. Wilkins is a writer of this class.   One touches New England when one comes in contact with her personages.

The author may give the setting definitely, as in " Ivanhoe," or he may leave the reader to infer it, as in "Sir Launfal," which is not set in England, as many suppose, but in the imagination of the poet.

The setting is often told from the life portrayed, from the scenery, from allusions made by the author, and from the characters employed. For example, the presence of Richard Coeur de Lion in "The Talisman" and "Ivanhoe" would alone locate these stories with reference to chivalry and the Crusades.

SUGGESTIVE QUESTIONS.

1. What must setting include? Why is it necessary?
2. How is it determined?
3. Name five stories which you know to have a definite setting.
4. Place in a list stories whose setting could be implied by the story itself. Illustrate.
5. Name a story which is set in chivalrous times; one which is set in Civil War times; one that belongs to this time.
6. Name a story whose setting is in the imagination, or not associated with any special time or place.
7. Locate in a general way these stories by the characters or the suggestions in them:

   a) Heroine, a Puritan maiden; hero, an old soldier. Scenes in colonial times.

   b) Chief character, a colored man; main scenes in a cotton field.

   c) The most prominent figure, a cowboy; the chief interest, gold-digging.

   d) Chief characters, a maiden and her lover. The story relates the sad experiences of exile.

8. What setting would you give a story of pioneer days in your own state?

9. In what setting would you place a story belonging to England in King Alfred's time?

10. Note the setting in "Silas Marner," in "Hard Times," in "The Talisman."

V. THE PLOT.

Essentials to the Mastery of Plot. — The first essential to the mastery of plot is mastery of the story as a whole. The plot is hidden in the story; we do not find it until we know the story. We are first attracted by character, by incident, by description; as the story advances all of these things take shape around a central idea. We start at a different point from the author. He started with plot — from within; we start with incident — from without. It is not till we get to the interior that we can find our way out as he found his way out.

All the class should master the story. Let one begin to tell it; another, and yet others, around the class, continue it. Stop short of monotony. Familiarity gives a content for the imagination to work upon. Just as the presence of any work of art influences the spiritual nature, so will familiarity with a masterpiece in story-telling enable it to influence the artistic sense. If the mind is stored with subject-matter, the power that would be used up in the acquisition of fact at an intense moment will be used in the higher emotions of aesthetic enjoyment: vistas will be opened; ideas formed; epochs in life made.

What the Plot Is. — The plot of a novel has been variously defined as "design applied to life"; as the chain of incidents without which the story could not exist; as that group of incidents which cluster about the life of the hero and which are absolutely essential to the story. The characteristics of a good plot are that it seems probable, has consistency of parts, or agrees with itself; that it is managed so as to hold the reader's attention throughout, and has provision for relief and climaxes. The plot is not that part of the story which thrusts itself upon the reader at first, but, rather, that part which is behind all and which appears through all, as the form of a Greek statue appears through the graceful drapery.

Unity of Plot. — The plot gets its unity from the hero or heroine. The plot interests have to do with the unfolding of the hero's character. Novels are classified upon the importance they place upon plot. (See chapter upon realism.) The distinction between plot and story should be kept clearly in mind. The plot is the skeleton or framework : the story the artistic production.

How to Find the Plot. — To find the plot, examine the incidents in the story; determine which are absolutely essential to the life of the story and which are used for the development or embellishment of these incidents. Having determined the plot incidents proper, determine which one out of the group forms the turning point or dramatic climax and those leading to and from it. The dramatic climax may be determined by its being the place where consequence sets in; the place from which one can look both ways—to beginning and to end. Here one sees the beginning (for want of a better phrase) begin to end, and the end begin to begin.

In writing the plot of given stories, only plot incidents proper should receive prominent mention. The developing incidents that lead to and from plot incidents proper ought to be mentioned by mere word or suggestion.

How to Write the Plot of a Given Story. — Let the hero be the unifying element for the various incidents. Underplots, or the plot within the plot, as the Cass story in "Silas Marner" and the Gloster episode in "King Lear," may receive separate attention.

PLOT OF "IVANHOE."

The following plot of "Ivanhoe" was written by a pupil in class in eight minutes, without notes. The limit of time for the class was ten minutes. The historical setting was given at a previous lesson.

"Cedric with Rowena, Ivanhoe's lady love, shelters for the night Prior Aymer, the Templar, his disguised son, and Isaac of York. At the tournament, soon after, the identity of the wounded but meritorious Ivanhoe is discovered, and Richard appears as the Black Knight. A plot of De Bracy to win Rowena caused him, with the Templar and De Boeuf, to capture in the forest and imprison in Torquilstone Cedric's company and the Jew's. De Bracy is refused by Rowena, and the Templar by Rebecca. The Black Knight and outlaws storm the castle, which is finally burned. Cedric, Ivanhoe, Rowena, Wamba, and the Jew are saved. De Bracy is banished, De Boeuf dies, and the Templar escapes with Rebecca to Templestowe, where she is accused of witchery and condemned to die, but is saved by Ivanhoe, who slays the Templar and who marries Rowena. Richard becomes king and pardons his false brother John. Rebecca and the Jew leave England."

SUGGESTIVE QUESTIONS.

1. Define a plot.
2. What preparation is absolutely necessary to the study of plot?

3. How does the reader approach the plot? The writer?

4. What are the characteristics of a good plot?

5. Is a complicated plot essential?

6. Name a writer who depends largely upon plot for his interest.   .

7. What class of fiction depends little upon plot? Illustrate.

8. Name as many stories as you can that sustain the interest independent of plot.

9. What is the dramatic climax or turning point of the story? How is it determined?

10. What direction is given about writing a plot? Give the plot of as many short stories as you can.

11. How do you distinguish between plot and story?

VI. THE STUDY OF INCIDENT.

The subject of incident is perhaps one of the most important in the study of fiction, since it is the point at which the reader enters the story. To be able to master the various incidents in a story is to be able to translate concrete or artistic expression into thought. One's appreciation increases in proportion to his power to go behind incident to thought. Here one realizes that the story-teller sees fit to show us the inner life of man by letting man act out that inner life, rather than by telling us in plain statement. For example, Scott does not tell that James Fitz-James loves animals, but he causes one to hear him mourn over his gallant gray. He does not say that James Fitz-James is bold, but one knows it upon hearing his speech when the Clan-Alpine men rise before him. And so one admires the modesty of Ellen Douglas when she pushes back her boat at the stranger's appearance, the nobility of the outlawed Roderick Dhu, and the high spirit of Malcolm Graeme swimming the lake — all of these deeds are admired in proportion to one's ability to translate them into thought. On the other hand, after one has learned to translate deed into thought, he proceeds from the inward to the outward, from thought to deed. When one knows a character to be possessed of certain attributes he can in a measure determine what that character will do under certain circumstances. This justifies the construction of futures for characters, — indeed, it is the very pivot upon which the active part of a story turns; it is this fact that lies at the bottom of plot and the various incidents used to develop it into a work of art.

In a well-appointed story, not only must everything that happens seem to grow naturally out of the situation, but it must seem to be the only thing that could happen under the circumstances. This gives rise to the classification of incidents, according to their importance, into *plot incident* proper and *developing incident*, each having an especial office of its own. The author knows his plot before he writes, but he frequently improvises means for its unfolding as the lines flow from his pen. These means for unfolding are called developing incidents; they lead to and from the plot incident to which they belong; they furnish the conditions and the successive steps of development for their plot incident. They furnish the cumulative effect necessary for the sub-climax, which a plot incident always forms. They hide the bare plot incidents and give the story grace and finish. A plot incident, with the group of developing incident which leads to it as a necessity arising out of certain causes, and from it so as to make results seem as natural as causes, forms an episode. An episode is a miniature story in itself, and, in its turn, acts as a developing incident in the progress of the plot as a whole. For example, the first plot incident proper in the " Lady of the Lake " is the meeting between Fitz-James and Ellen. Leading up to this it is necessary to have the chase, necessary for Fitz-James to out-distance his companions, to lose his horse and his way, and to blow his horn.

All of these are developing incidents leading up to the plot incident proper, — James's meeting with Ellen Douglas. The developing incidents leading away from this take Fitz-James to the home of Roderick Dhu, provide him his night's lodging, and send him away next morning. This group of incidents forms an episode of which the climax is the plot incident proper.

Incidents may be further classified by their kind into dramatic or commonplace; into character incident or into incident purely artistic; also into incident used for relief, for foreshadowing, for contrast; to set forth custom or superstition, and to give any information which the author wishes to convey.

A Dramatic Incident. — A dramatic incident or situation is better known by illustration and comparison than by definition. For example, two boys are walking quietly to school on a snowy morning. This is a commonplace incident: there are hundreds of boys walking to school on this morning. The two boys come to a slope, when one falls back of the other, raises his arms in the air, and cries to the one who is in front of him, " Now, say your prayers ! " He suddenly rushes forward and pushes the front boy into the snowdrift. This is dramatic. It is a commonplace incident changed to a dramatic incident; it shows more feeling, gives a more vivid picture, is fraught with greater results. It is accompanied by dramatic conversation, though this is not always the case with dramatic situations. One may be stricken with great grief or surprise and present a most dramatic situation without speaking a word. Tableaux are dramatic situations which explain themselves without words. Dramatic situations often represent crises in the course of lives or events.

How to Study Incident. — An incident may be studied by determining its kind; if it be dramatic, by noting whether or not it is accompanied by dramatic conversation, and by the outcome. If it be a plot incident proper, decide where it belongs with regard to turning point — is it before or after? What is its importance in the outcome? If it be a developing incident, what plot incident does it lead to or away from? If it be a character incident, look behind it into the motive out of which it sprang, and determine how it portrays the character. Does it show character growth in its beginning? in its advancement? or does it illustrate character full grown? If an incident be for purely artistic purposes, justify its presence in the light of the story of which it is a part. Learn to group into one episode all the developing incidents that lead directly to and from a plot incident; then it will be easy to trace the development of interest, to appreciate the artistic value of little things, and to realize the inevitableness of the final outcome.

Nothing fixes the study of incident and plot in the mind so well as an attempt to write a plot. The following plot was selected from a lesson assigned two weeks in advance, to be written at home. The directions were: "Bring to class four paragraphs upon an *imaginary* novel of your own writing. Let paragraph I contain the title, author, size, publisher, price. Paragraph II, the setting, including time, place, and main characters. Paragraph III, the plot. Paragraph IV, comment upon the book after the manner of press comment. For hints, see the *Literary News, Literary World, Literary Digest, The Critic, The Dial,* and other papers of like character. Nothing but the four paragraphs need be written. The rest is to be imagined."

(STUDENT'S PAPER.)

I. *" Witty Dan."*

A book that will create considerable comment among readers of juvenile fiction is "Witty Dan," the latest work of Hendricks Nemo. (In one volume, cloth bound, price 78 cts., and published by the Nihil Publishing Co., Nominloco, Ind.)

II. *Setting.*

The scenes of this story are laid at Indianapolis, and the incidents mentioned in it occurred during the administration of Governor Matthews.

III. *Plot.*

Dan Trowbridge, through the unjust imprisonment of his father as an embezzler, has to leave school to earn a support for the family, He is serving as elevator boy at the State Capitol, when sent in an emergency to the Denison Hotel for a paper. The hotel is on fire, but Dan does his errand through smoke and flame. He picks up a sealed envelope that lies on the floor as he comes out. The governor commends him for his bravery, and two months after, through the contents of the envelope that

Dan picked up in the burning hotel, his father is pardoned and given a position. Dan is sent to school and the family made happy.

IV. *Comment.*

Mr. Nemo certainly deserves much credit for the skill and talent he displays in the writing of this novel. He succeeds in giving a true and interesting account of life in the metropolis of Indiana. His descriptions of the buildings for which Indianapolis is famous are the clearest and most accurate ever written.

There is also in this story a thrilling account of the row which took place in the State House over the Fee and Salary Bill early in March, 1895, and the author necessarily strips bare and holds up to the reader the corruption of the legislature by which the bill was considered. The great Denison House fire of February, 1895, likewise receives a thrilling description, and Mr. Nemo gives to the Indianapolis Fire Department deserved praise.

Throughout the story there runs a strain of sparkling wit and humor. The language, indeed, is so simple that very young readers will have no difficulty in comprehending the plot. This book, furthermore, brings out the

better characteristics of the American boy,
through the steadfastness of Dan Trowbridge,
whose example will exert a most ennobling
influence over the readers of this book.

QUESTIONS.

(Based upon the foregoing text.)

Incident. — 1. Why is an understanding of
incident important in the study of fiction?

2. How does the novelist tell of life?

3. Mention incidents that set forth certain
attributes.

4. Assume an attribute and tell how the per-
son would act in an emergency.

5. How must every incident appear in every
well-appointed story?

6. How are incidents classified with regard
to their importance in the plot?

7. What is a developing incident? How does
it perform its office?

8. How do developing incidents stand related
to the entire story?

9. What is a plot incident?

10. What is an episode? Name episodes in
stories which you have read.

11. Write a plot of the "Lady of the Lake."
Indicate same by diagram. (Any story
may be substituted.)

12. Treat the incidents in the episode of the
combat between Fitz-James and Roderick Dhu as follows:

  a) Make a list of the developing incidents leading to the climax of
the episode.

  b) Designate the climax of episode.

  c) Make a list of the developing incidents leading from the climax.
The same may be indicated by
diagram.

13. Give examples of character incident. Incident for purpose of relief. For foreshadowing. To set forth custom or
superstition.

14. What is a dramatic incident? How characterized?

15. With what may a dramatic incident or
moment often be accompanied? In what
instances may a dramatic situation be
unaccompanied?

16. Illustrate how a commonplace incident may
be changed into a dramatic incident or
situation. Give illustrations from life
as well as from books.

17. Mention some dramatic situations that you
have observed in life. What use could
be made of them?

18. Give directions for studying an incident.

19. Select some incident, construct therefrom
a plot, and write four paragraphs as
follows : —

     Par. I. Title, author, publisher, price,
size. (The writer may use an
assumed name.)

     Par. II. Setting.

     Par. III. Plot.

     Par. IV. Comment, after the manner
of press comment.

NOTE. — See foregoing exercise by student
for question 19.

VII. CHARACTER STUDY.

Character study is the life of a novel.
Through it one enters into the active arena
and becomes acquainted with all that interests
humanity. A study of character gives pleasure
and leads to insight. Through it the names
on the pages of the story become alive to the
reader. Character study brings one to a reali-
zation of the struggle that may take place in
a human soul. This is eminently true in the

struggle between knighthood and manhood in the breast of Sir Kenneth in the banner scene in "The Talisman." It strengthens one's will to see this knight stand before Richard and choose death with honor to escape with disgrace, although four ways are open to him for escape. The powers of sympathy and love are called forth by the feeble-minded weaver of Raveloe, and the reader better understands Eliot's quotation from Wordsworth on the title-page.

How to Study Character. — The characters in a story may be idealized or natural; they may be consistent or inconsistent with regard to the part they play in the story. A character may be studied:

1. By its innate tendencies, or its inner promptings, independent of any external influence.

2. By its environment, or surroundings, and the way in which it has overcome them or been overcome by them.

3. In the light of heredity, or inherited traits.

4. By its manifestations of willing, thinking, feeling.

5. By its achievements, or what it has accomplished in the light of its effort and opportunity, and by the development it makes.

6. By noting all that a character says and does, all that is said and done to him, and all that is said about him.

7. By noting the dominant motive of his life, whether it be love, hate, revenge, a sense of duty, selfishness, or forgiveness.

8. A character may be studied by putting one's self in another's place; by being the apple-woman, the newsboy, the boot-black for a time, and looking at life through their eyes. Be a beggar, a millionaire, a master, or a slave, and imagine what you would do in each situation.

Upon being asked how he studied character, a boy said: "I do more than my directions state. I take my character out of the book and live with him and walk with him; he becomes my comrade. I grow to know him so well that I can tell what he would do under other circumstances than those in which the author placed him. I even ask him what he thinks of me and of certain things."

The following character studies were written in class without notes in ten minutes.

REBECCA.

(Written by a boy of sixteen.)

Not in the whole of Scott's fiction is there another Rebecca. We like Rebecca and admire her—why? I like Rebecca so much that I think less of Ivanhoe because he did not love her more and marry her instead of Rowena. And I like that fierce Templar more because of his passion for Rebecca, even though it was such a rude passion. She had such wonderful self-control and will-power and bravery. Think how, though she loved Ivanhoe with all the depth of her nature, she never showed it, never resented his loving another. Think how she preferred death to dishonor; how she would have cast herself from the dizzy turret. The character she showed in that interview would have given her a place in the ranks of the truly great. Hers was the stuff of which martyrs are made.

NOTE. —This sketch shows that an intensive study of fiction tends rather to foster than to crush spontaneity; it is a valuable illustration, because the personality of the writer pulsates through every sentence, giving it life. The second sketch shows more of class drill.

SALADIN: A CHARACTER STUDY.

(Written by a girl.)

Saladin possessed all the prudence and fore-thought of a monarch in the truest sense, and also the nobility and generosity which might grace any name.   He showed all the attributes which we give to the Christian, while Richard, on the other hand, seems to display the head-strongness and fiery temper which we com-monly assign to a heathen.   He had all the wiry agility of his race, and it stood him in good stead in his combat with Kenneth.   It was pure generosity and nobility of character which led him to exercise the healing art upon Richard.   Though humble as a physician, when stung by Richard's ingratitude he assumes a lofty and kingly bearing.   What was more noble than his treatment of Kenneth, now his slave!   But Saladin is seen to greatest ad-vantage in his own camp and surrounded by believers of his own faith, where his native courtesy and kindness mark him one of nature's kings.   In all his disguises he is ever the same, loyal to his faith, true and even generous in his treatment of enemies, and faithful to his friends.

(Time, 10 min.)

Suggestive Exercises.

1. Bring to class a study of some character from the "Lady of the Lake" or from any other books that you know.
2. Bring a character study from life.
3. Name book characters that are marked by their will-power, by a tender conscience; that have powerful intellect. Prove by citing your authority.
4. What characters have you found idealized? What characters realistic? What saints? Sinners?
5. Howells speaks of letting conduct do its "unsermonized office." What do you understand by the expression?
6. Is Roderick Dhu idealized? Ellen Douglas?
7. Tell how you study a character from life.
8. Mention a list of book characters that are very real to you. Locate them.
9. What quality of character indicated by the hoarding of money for its own sake? Illustrate. By the founding of educational institutions?
10. Who is your favorite book character? Why?

11. Do you prefer that a character should be idealized or portrayed exactly as in real life? Give reasons.
12. Does nobility of character belong to any special rank in life? Whose books have set forth this question plainly?
13. How are the characters of Sissy Jupe and Mr. M'Choakumchild each brought out when Sissy is examined upon political economy by Mr. M'Choakumchild?
14. Make a list of character incidents in the novel you are studying and trace, in a general way, each incident to the mental impulse out of which it sprang.

VIII. METHOD.

An author's method is his manner of telling his story, and may often be determined by the reader if he put to himself such questions as these : How does this author tell his story? Is his style pleasing? his narrative straightforward? Does he proportion his use of description and narration well? Does he comment upon his characters and tell the reader what to see, or does he speak only through his characters and let the reader see for himself? Does he depict life as it is or as he thinks it ought to be ; *i.e.*, is his story romantic or realistic ? Does he set forth the democratic or the aristocratic phase of life ? That of the saint or the sinner ? Is his canvas large or small ? Compare Tolstoï's " Peace and War " and Wilkins's " Pembroke." Is his book pervaded by a literary atmosphere through allusion, and does he take the reader to his study, or is it pervaded by an outdoor atmosphere, taking the reader under the open sky, to the fields and woods, to listen to the lowing of the kine or the song of the brook and the birds ?

Wherein does the author's strength lie ? Is it in handling plot, as shown in Stockton's stories ? Management of detail, as in Wilkins ? Portrayal of character, as in Eliot ? Description of scene and event, as in Hardy ? In power of setting forth dramatic situation, as in Scott ? Is he picturesque, *i.e.*, does he state facts by situation and scene, by suggestion and implication, or does he use direct statement ?

EXERCISES.

1. Mention some books in which you once skipped the long descriptions. Look at these books again and see if you can tell why.

2. Mention the most straightforward narrative that you know.

3. Mention authors that comment upon the characters.

4. Mention authors that let their characters do all the talking.

5. Mention writers that depict high life.

6. Mention authors that depict lowly life.

7. In what books have you found saints? sinners?

8. Where have you found allusions that showed the learning of the author and that gave the book a literary atmosphere?

9. What books have taken you to outdoor life?

10. Make a list of ten facts that are told by situation, giving :

    a. Situation. *b.* Facts. *c.* From what taken.

11. Make a list of ten suggestions used to convey facts, giving :

    a. Suggestion. *b.* Facts. *c.* Place.

12. Make a list of ten scenes that convey facts, giving:

    a. Scene. *b.* Facts conveyed.

13. Give examples of delicate humor in fiction.

14. Give examples of pathos in fiction.

IX. PURPOSE.

The purpose of an author may be to forward a cause, as in " Uncle Tom's Cabin "; to set forth a theory, as in " Looking Backward "; to picture a bygone time, as in " Ivanhoe ": or it may be to depict life pure and simple, as in " A Modern Instance "; or simply to entertain. The purpose of the author determines in a degree the classification of his art.

If an author's purpose be purely artistic, *i.e.*, if he wishes only to portray life faithfully as it is, his work is realistic.

If he uses the story to set forth his particular views, his work is philosophic.

If his purpose is to picture some historic personage, event, or time, his work is historical.

If he wishes to entertain by setting forth any theme with extravagant treatment, by centering the interest in the story, and by giving a prominent part to love, his work is romantic.

Any two or more of these classes of fiction may be combined. A work may be philosophic-realism, historical-romance, etc.

EXERCISE.

Place in lists, as indicated below, as many stories as you know that will illustrate the headings. The same story may come under more than one heading.

1. Stories that give a faithful portrayal of life without any particular lesson. (Realistic.)

   a. Author.   *b.* Story.   *c.* What life pictured.

2. Stories that set forth some particular view of the author.   (Philosophic.)

   a. Author.   *b.* Story.   *c.* View of what?

3. Stories that picture a past time, event, or personage.   (Historical.)

   a. Author.   *b.* Story.   *c.* Time, event, or personage.

4. Stories that depend upon plot.   (Romantic.)

   a. Author.   *b.* Story.

5. Stories independent of plot.   (Realistic.)

   a. Author.   *b.* Story.

6. Stories that contain highly dramatic moments.

   a. Author.   *b.* Story.   *c.* Moments.

X. COMMENT.

Comment is a very general term; it may give the student's personal impressions concerning a work; it may give any information he wishes to convey about it, or it may be of the nature of criticism commending or noting faults, according to the merits or demerits of the book. Sometimes comment includes plot, setting, mention of character, and critical estimate upon the literary quality of a story. A good comment indicates a high quality of mental power on the part of the one who makes it.

Examples of comment are found in book notices, briefs of books, and short book reviews in the *Literary News,* the *Literary Digest, The Bookman, The Dial,* the *Review of Reviews, The Nation,* and the various periodicals.

The following is a fair sample:

Harraden, Beatrice. "Ships that Pass in the Night." Authorized American ed. N. Y., G. Putnam's Sons, 1891. 7 + 235 p. S. cl., $1.

The story takes place at Petershof, a winter resort for consumptives in the Swiss Mountains. The chief characters are Robert Allitsen, a rich young Englishman, whose days are numbered, and Bernardine Holme, an intellectual young English girl, who has broken down under a strain of work in teaching, writing, etc. Their story is a simple, everyday one, the novelty being in the telling and in the many shrewd and philosophical remarks of the writer, betraying a deep study of life and human nature. The apt title is taken from Longfellow "Ships that pass in a night, and speak each other in passing," etc.

SUGGESTIVE QUESTIONS.

1. What may be contained in comment?
2. Where can good comment be found?
3. Note the foregoing example and separate it into the parts of the story as herein studied.
4. Criticise the student's comment found on page 39 of this book.
5. Write a comment upon a story with which you are familiar.
6. Comment upon the characters in the story.
7. Report upon a number of comments examined and find those in which plots are given.
8. Make comment upon the descriptions in a certain book.
9. Comment upon the method and purpose of some particular story.
10. Comment upon the comment you last made after laying it away for a time.

XI. EXERCISES ILLUSTRATING THE DEVELOPMENT OF POWER IN THE STUDY OF FICTION.

An intensive study of fiction, as of other forms of literature, leads to a conscious acquisition of power; power used in the same sense as in physics, — the ability to do work in a given time; power not only to handle a book and tell what is in it, but power to do this promptly, easily, and in a pleasing manner. Power in the study of literature may be included under three heads: the power to acquire, the power to interpret, and the power to express. Any one of these may serve to check the others. Interpretation will keep one from being an echo through disproportionate acquisition. Both interpretation and acquisition aid in expression.

Power to Acquire. — Power to acquire is the ability to make a thing one's own; it depends largely upon memory to fix in the mind the form, the exact words, the arrangement of words, and even the punctuation. It enables one to gather and carry facts. The anthropologist says that the ear has almost lost its place in education. As much might be said

of the memory. *Intelligent* committing to
memory is fixing the attention; it is learning
an art product in the terms of art; it is sub-
mitting to the creative impulse of the author
and thus increasing aesthetic enjoyment. Exercise of the memory is the best preparation
for the intensive study of literature. It makes
way for the rhythmic swing, beauty of imagery,
and the suggested subtleties of thought. The
memory keeps on hand data ready for comparison with new facts. An exercise of memory
enables one to classify as one reads or listens,
and the best of all its results is in the cumulative
effect arising from the thought-habit which it
forms. It should be employed in fiction as in
other forms of literature.

Power to Interpret. — Power to interpret is
constantly called into play in the study of fiction. Interpretation goes on during acquisition,
but it can be the dominant activity. To interpret is to resolve language into the thought of
which it is a symbol. This is from the point
of view of the reader or listener. From the
point of view of the writer it is to concrete
one's own thought into the proper word symbols. The interpreter must see the masterpiece
from the interior, from the author's point of
view; he must also see it from the exterior,

the reader's point of view; then from the two
he must resolve it into the elements of his own
thought, and send it forth with the stamp of
his own personality upon it.

Power to Express.—Power to express is the
test of one's ability to assimilate. It is not to
reproduce in the original form, but to give
forth what has been acquired and interpreted
in the living personality of the interpreter.
Successful expression has vitality: it carries
the stamp of the writer's integrity to his own
impressions and his respect for saying a thing
after the manner of his own genius; it shows
that matter has been mixed with mind. Expression as herein used includes oral and written speech.

Oral expression is one of the demands of
modern education. One must be able to speak
as well as to write; one must be able to think
and talk upon one's feet. Under oral expression comes class criticism, to which a separate
space will be given.

One way of vitalizing expression is to give
it variety,—to have the same thing looked at
and spoken of in manifold ways.

ILLUSTRATION OF THE WAY IN WHICH VARI-
ETY OF EXPRESSION MAY BE SECURED.

Variety of Expression. — NOTE. — The following paper is taken from a lesson prepared at
home. The pupils were asked to select any
dramatic moment in "Ivanhoe" and then in
the fewest words possible they were, first, to
give a plain account of the moment selected;
second, they were to write it in pictorial language; and, third, they were to comment upon
the moment.

(STUDENT'S PAPER.)

SCENE BETWEEN ISAAC OF YORK AND DE BOEUF.

I. *In Plain Language.*

Front de Boeuf entered the dungeon of the
Jew, accompanied by the Saracen slaves, and
with threats of death by torture induced Isaac
to promise a ransom of one thousand pounds of
silver. But on learning the fate of his daughter he recalled his promise, and preferred to
die rather than ransom himself without her.
The Norman lord and his men were preparing
to carry out their fiendish plan when inter-
rupted by the bugle.

(77 words.)

II. *In Pictorial Language.*

See the Jew abjectly crouching in the corner!
Dank odors rise on every side. See the rusty
chains upon the floor, the empty hearth, and
windows barred! The door is opened. In
comes De Boeuf with his companions. Isaac
cowers before the Norman lord. What! A
thousand pounds! Does he refuse? Ah, see
the glowing grate, the bars of iron, the cruel
stones! He can but yield, and does. But
what! His daughter gone? He will not pay.
They blow the fire; they strip him bare; they
seize his aged limbs! But stop! A bugle
blows. Isaac is saved.

(90 words.)

III. *Comment.*

This dramatic interview between De Boeuf
and Isaac impresses upon the reader two points:
the fiendish cruelty of the Norman and the
patient affection of the Jew. The setting for
such an effect is admirable. The dark dungeon, the black stones, the glowing furnace are
almost symbolic of the mind of the baron. The
Jew's ready submission, his agreement to the
ransom, well sets off his later resistance and
preference of death to his daughter's dishonor.

The abrupt bugle is a welcome relief from the anticipated death of Isaac and from the high dramatic tension throughout the scene.

(98 words.)

NOTE. — Counting words calls the student's attention to the use of every word, and gives the teacher an idea of what limit may be placed upon paragraph lengths. This exercise may be further used to call attention to proportion. It is well to lead a learner to see that he must get somewhere. He often starts well, but never reaches any place.

Fiction affords further opportunity for variety in expression in studying the discourse forms of soliloquy, monologue, and dialogue, and in changing one form into another. The following soliloquy changed to a monologue will illustrate the point.

DIRECTIONS. — Copy a soliloquy found in "The Talisman." Change it into a monologue.

(STUDENT'S PAPER.)

SCENE. — De Vaux discusses the merits of the Saracen physician (134).

I. *Soliloquy.*

(From "The Talisman.")

Wherefore, it is in no sense impossible that this El Hakim, with this his cure, or seeming

cure, wrought on the body of the Scottish
squire, may mean nothing but a trick, to
which he of the Leopard may be accessory,
and wherein the Bishop of Tyre, prelate as
he is, may have some share.

II. (*The Soliloquy changed to a Monologue.*)

Strange, very strange, indeed. From the
case of this poor squire it would seem that this
infidel leech does possess certain powers. And
this El Hakim, as he calls himself, would try
his art upon King Richard? For that purpose
was he sent and by the unbelieving Soldan
himself. Richard, indeed, is all anxiety to
have him do so. He trusts this Eastern prince
as if he were his brother. But this may be a
plot, an attempt on the life of Richard; the
Eastern conjurors are adepts in the art of poison-
ing. The Scot, who recommends him so, could
he be traitor? Would bravery and treason so
combine? Yet I have ever found them fair
and false, these Scotchmen. Then the Bishop
of Tyre — why his advice and willingness?
Why his perturbation when I told him of the
Scot's return? But he is a prelate. But
Richard is a king. When kings are being
poisoned does the rank of prelate signify im-

peccability?   Verily, treason is all about me.
I must be on my guard, indeed.

VOCABULARY.

As language is the medium for literary expression, words are needed both for thought and
for the expression of thought.   One's vocabulary
should increase as his thoughts increase.   Aside
from devices placed in books for the enlarge-
ment of a vocabulary, no author should be
intensively studied without giving attention to
the words he uses.   Is his a fact vocabulary
like Defoe's?   Is it poetic like Ruskin's?   Is
it simple Saxon like Bunyan's, or of classic
origin like De Quincey's?

After comparing the same number of words
in the vocabularies of Scott, Ruskin, De Quincey, and Defoe, the following conclusions were
reached by the pupils :   Scott's vocabulary is
largely a fact vocabulary and employs a large
number of action words in its many dramatic
situations.   Scott's vocabulary has fewer modi-
fiers than Ruskin's and more than Defoe's,
showing that Scott's style is less ornate than
Ruskin's and more embellished than Defoe's.
Scott uses many connectives — hence, long,
loose, or compound sentences; Scott inserts

Latin phrases. The language of the essayist De Quincey differs from that of the romanticist Scott, thus showing that the form of discourse determines, in a measure, the vocabulary of a writer. Scott's sentences are longer than Emerson's, and the suggestiveness of Scott's expression is found in the use of epithet.

CRITICISM.

Self Criticism. — A great help to expression is the power to criticise one's own work. Especially is this true in the papers prepared in the study of fiction. This is helpful in the writing of plot, dramatic situation, and character study. One can ask one's self with profit : Is my exercise grammatically correct in word forms and agreement? in sentence structure and sentence connection? Is it rhetorically correct in diction? in clearness? in paragraph structure and paragraph transition? Is it true on the fact side? Have I proportioned my exercise right as to parts? as to emphasis of points? Have I gotten somewhere or lost myself in detail? Is my exercise up to the level of the piece I am treating? Have I brought out any of the subtleties of meaning?

Class Criticism. — As has been said, class or oral criticism deserves a special place. Class criticism cultivates the power to listen, the power to think while listening, also the power to judge and discriminate. It creates standards of literary expression, leads to appreciation of the good and the beautiful and the true in letters. It carries home truths that would be felt in no other way. Every one who offers a criticism must give it in a kind manner. No indefinite criticisms are to be permitted in class. The one criticised learns to side with his critic, and thus all are helped. The points to listen for are correctness of expression, of facts, the bringing out of new facts, and the interpretation of the subject-matter.

Cultivation of the Imagination. — The cultivation of the imagination may be also helped by selecting passages conveying the most vivid impressions and then noting how the impression is conveyed. Is it by suggestion or inference, independent of epithet or figure? Is it by figure? Is it by epithet? Give examples of all these ways; *e.g.*, "A tear stood in the eye of the Saxon," "The rose of Palestine," "The scraggly oak." Words are hereby vitalized and used in their literary sense. It is well to see that words have an etymological meaning, a dictionary meaning, and an associated meaning. The imagination can be kept active by the subject-matter of fiction in this way.

XII. A WORD ABOUT REALISM.

Perhaps no word troubles the student of fiction at the present day more than the word "realism." The following pages attempt to give only a few of the distinctive features of realistic fiction written in the English language.

Realism is known by its portrayal of life as it is, as opposed to life as it ought to be. Realism gives us individuals rather than types; it portrays life in parts or instances rather than in wholes. In realism the reader always feels that the writer has his eyes upon the object which he describes.

Realism is unlike romanticism in that it depends less upon plot and dramatic situations, and follows, rather, the natural course of life and events. The interest in realism centers upon the play of character, while the interest in romanticism centers upon the development of story. The success of realism depends largely upon the significance of the details selected. Professor Raleigh says of realism that "it is the microscope laying bare the details of daily life, and superseding the telescope that brought the heavens nearer to the earth."

Realism in relation to knowledge is the outgrowth of the spirit of scientific investigation; in relation to literature it is the outgrowth of the spirit of criticism; in its relation to life and art it is the outgrowth of the spirit of democracy.

Realism is as old as fiction. Literature showed a marked tendency to realism in the Passion. Miracle, Saint, and Morality plays of the church from the twelfth to the sixteenth centuries. These plays left the church altars for the open fields; the parts in them were played by special actors instead of by the clergy who had before played them. The creation of Adam often took place on the stage. Models were taken from real life, and while these plays were yet performed in the church, realistic details represented by the live child, the actual manger, and the lighted candle were used.

In 1362 William Langland wrote his "Piers, the Plowman." He drew his materials from life. He might have been swayed by literary themes, for he lived in the time of Chaucer.

and Wickliffe was his friend. Froissart was at
the time chronicling the court life of France ;
the Meistersingers had established their guilds
in Germany, and in Italy Boccaccio had given
the Decameron and Petrarch the Sonnet form
to the literary world. These facts enhance
the value of the realistic tendency found in
Langland. He takes his reader from the courts
to the Malvern Hills, to see in a vision a "fair
field full of folk." Langland himself is the
plowman in the vision. Sowing and reaping,
tilling the soil and husbandry assume dignity ;
there is confidence in the ongoing processes of
nature. Along with knight and parson we
hear the cook crying out, " Hote pyes, hote."
Langland is also realistic in his independence
of plot ; to change his scene he invents no
situations, but simply says : " and the scene
shifts." Along with Langland, realism is also
found in Chaucer's " Canterbury Tales." It
was a mixed company that started out from
the Tabard Inn with the great humorist story-
teller. One laughs and feels with them all,
and, whether Chaucer means to hold his characters up for ridicule or admiration, they are
none the less interesting and none the less real.

There is a space of more than two hundred
years from Chaucer to Thomas Nash, the first

true realist in English prose fiction. Nash
was an original writer and believed that every
man should express himself in his own vein.
He led the picaresque school in England.
This school was founded in Spain about 1553.
Translations found their way into the neigh-
boring countries, and their appearance in England marked an epoch in English fiction. The
picaresque school is named from the picaro, —
the rogue, — who seemed always to be the
leading character in this style of story. The
picaro is set forth as a creature of caprice and
fate, and the part assigned him calls for little
conscience and less heart. The scenes are all
vivid and awaken the interest of the reader in
spite of himself. Nash's "Jack Wilton" is a
true picaresque tale, and is the ancestor of
many novels which lack the ancestral vigor.

The printing press had been used nearly
one hundred years when "Jack Wilton" was
written, and during this time the existing
English novels and the translations into English from French, Spanish, and German writers
were multiplied.

From Thomas Nash's "Jack Wilton," in
1594, to Richardson's "Pamela," in 1740, there
is another space—nearly one hundred and fifty
years this time. One stops with Richardson

more because he is called the "father of the English novel" than because of his contribution to realism. He belongs to the school in fiction which Sidney represents in poetry,—that of sentiment; but he contributed to prose fiction the naturalness peculiar to the letter form, and gave a microscopic analysis of sentiment and a minute portrayal of womanly character. The novel is now well born, and Bunyan, Defoe, and Fielding come near together, each making his especial contribution. Bunyan gave lessons in the handling of character. It is said that he gave to the England of the seventeenth century its one true picture of human life and victory. Defoe was the follower of Nash in the picaresque style. A taste for fact rather than fancy had set in. The positive temper had sprung up. Defoe's language was fact language; he made no attempt at embellishment, and he excelled in the realistic treatment of his theme. As Richardson taught heart analysis, Bunyan taught character portrayal, and Defoe the handling of realistic detail, so Fielding taught the value of dramatic situation and complicated plot. His "Tom Jones" is not called a book, but a man. Underneath all its coarseness there is in "Tom Jones" a healthy return to nature.

Fielding hated shams and hypocrites and placed much reliance upon the bottom facts in human nature. He began in satire and ended in reform.

In passing from Fielding's "Tom Jones," 1749, to Jane Austen's "Pride and Prejudice," in 1812, fiction has come into the modern world, — our own world. The revival of learning which marked the Elizabethan age, with its long line of immortals, led by Shakespeare, Bacon, Spenser, Sidney, and Marlowe, has been passed. The novelists herein previously mentioned have played their part. The first draft of Waverley has for some time been lying in Sir Walter's chest, and the " Lady of the Lake " is about to appear. The Reformation has been voiced in the writings of Milton and Bunyan and the age of the Restoration has followed. John Dryden, Sir Isaac Newton, and Sir Christopher Wren have advanced criticism, philosophy, and architecture; a return to classic style has been made by Pope, Addison, and Steele, and these in their turn have been followed by Burns, Byron, Shelley, and Wordsworth, setting forth the spirit of the Revolution. So one is justified in saying that Jane Austen is a modern; she looked out upon the modern world and came under the same influences that sway the people now living. "Pride and Prejudice" is realistic in its narrowness of scope, in its lack of complicated plot, and in that it sets forth clearly and fully a limited section of life. It attempts to hold up no ideals; it deals for the most part with middle-class people; it has in it no literary atmosphere suggested either by the characters or by the author's allusions. And yet one forgets that he is reading a book; he feels as if he were making a visit among people in whom he had a human interest. He finds himself scheming with the fond mother in her matchmaking interests for her daughters five. Howells calls Jane Austen the "divine Jane," and wonders "how people who had once known her simple veracity and refined perfection could enjoy anything less perfect." He says: "She was the first and the last of English novelists to handle material with entire truthfulness, and because she did this she is worthy to be matched with the great Scandinavian and Slavic and Latin artists."

After Jane Austen, Charles Dickens and George Eliot open the gates of common life. Democracy has a new meaning, or its meaning has penetrated fiction. The priest in the tower asking, "Where art thou, Lord?" has heard in audible words: "Down here among my people." The writers of realism are to-day legion in number, and so varied is this phase of fiction that many volumes baffle the classifiers.

Realism has been employed for various purposes. George Eliot has used it as the medium for conveying great lessons upon the redemptive power of love in "Silas Marner," of renunciation in "Romola," and of fate in "Mill on the Floss." Thomas Hardy has proved it capable of setting forth tragedy in "Tess." George Meredith has found it equally capable for the representation of comedy in his "Egoist." Mrs. Ward has used realism to advance her theories of social reform. Howells has made it the vehicle of the realistic commonplace, and Mary E. Wilkins of the minute. Realism is found discussing all questions that engage the attention at the present time. It selects its characters from all stations in life; saint and sinner, rich and poor file along its pages. One writer lets the reader see the vision by himself; another takes the reader by the hand and points out to him the significance of the view.

The exponents of realism in the United States are led by W. D. Howells, Mary E.

Wilkins, and Henry James. Howells is at the head of writers of "artistic realism," or that species of fiction which has no object whatever but the picturing of life. Mary E. Wilkins is most truly realistic in "Pembroke." She reminds one of Jane Austen in her narrow scope and clear-cut figures. Henry James has but slight hold upon Americans on account of his love for foreign countries. Beers says: "He looks at America with the eyes of a foreigner, and at Europe with the eyes of an American."

Some critics say that realism has reached its limit, while others see a future for fiction only along this line.

XIII. SOME BOOKS SUITABLE FOR STUDY IN SECONDARY SCHOOLS.

The following list is in no way exhaustive, but the books contained in it are believed to be unobjectionable in quality and tone. There is a sufficiently wide range for selection, since the time allowed for fiction on a secondary school program is too short for the study of more than four books at most. The principles guiding the selection of novels for study should be based upon the particular

needs of the class. The same books may not
of necessity be the best ones year after year;
but it would seem advisable for the classes
to study such works as will give them a clear
idea of the differences between romanticism
and realism, — works not too difficult for the
students to discover for themselves these differences. Scott is still the pattern romancer,
and Wilkins and Eliot furnish examples of
artistic and philosophic realism; or in other
words, Eliot states the lessons of philosophy
which she wishes her stories to convey, while
Wilkins seems to write only to give a faithful
picture of life and to let that picture tell its
own story.

The novels used in the course out of which
this book grew were: "The Talisman," "Ivanhoe," "Silas Marner," and "Hard Times."
While the first book was being read, the principles herein set forth were applied to the
"Lady of the Lake," with which the students
were already familiar. No book should be
studied in class until it has been made familiar
as a whole.

NOTE. — The following list is named without reference
to any special classification.

ALDRICH, T. B. — Marjorie Daw.
ALLEN, J. L. — Flute and Violin. (Kentucky.)

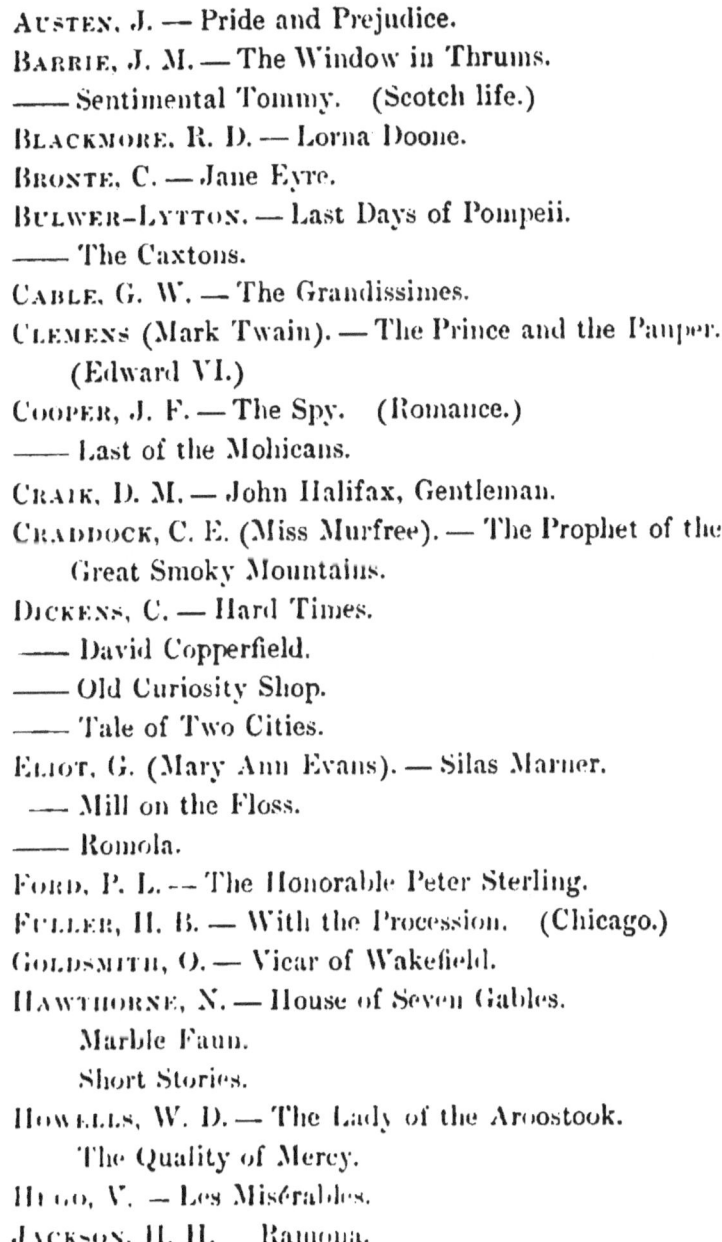

AUSTEN, J. — Pride and Prejudice.
BARRIE, J. M. — The Window in Thrums.
—— Sentimental Tommy.   (Scotch life.)
BLACKMORE, R. D. — Lorna Doone.
BRONTE, C. — Jane Eyre.
BULWER-LYTTON. — Last Days of Pompeii.
—— The Caxtons.
CABLE, G. W. — The Grandissimes.
CLEMENS (Mark Twain). — The Prince and the Pauper.
   (Edward VI.)
COOPER, J. F. — The Spy.   (Romance.)
—— Last of the Mohicans.
CRAIK, D. M. — John Halifax, Gentleman.
CRADDOCK, C. E. (Miss Murfree). — The Prophet of the
   Great Smoky Mountains.
DICKENS, C. — Hard Times.
—— David Copperfield.
—— Old Curiosity Shop.
—— Tale of Two Cities.
ELIOT, G. (Mary Ann Evans). — Silas Marner.
   —— Mill on the Floss.
—— Romola.
FORD, P. L. — The Honorable Peter Sterling.
FULLER, H. B. — With the Procession.   (Chicago.)
GOLDSMITH, O. — Vicar of Wakefield.
HAWTHORNE, N. — House of Seven Gables.
   Marble Faun.
   Short Stories.
HOWELLS, W. D. — The Lady of the Aroostook.
   The Quality of Mercy.
HUGO, V. — Les Misérables.
JACKSON, H. H.   Ramona.

JAMES, H. — A Portrait of a Lady.

KINGSLEY, C. — Hypatia.

—— Westward Ho.

KIPLING, R. — Short Stories.

McDONALD, G. — Robert Falconer.

MITCHELL, S. W. — Hugh Wynne.

READE, C. — The Cloister and the Hearth.

—— Put Yourself in his Place.

SCOTT, SIR W. — The Talisman.

—— Ivanhoe.

—— The Lady of the Lake.

—— Woodstock. (All of Scott's novels can be recommended.)

STEVENSON, R. L. — Treasure Island.

—— Kidnapped.

—— The Wrecker.

STOCKTON, F. — The Hundredth Man. (Good for plot and humor.)

STOWE, H. B. — Uncle Tom's Cabin.

THACKERAY, W. M. — Vanity Fair.

—— Henry Esmond.

—— The Newcomes.

TOLSTOI. — Master and Man.

WEYMAN, S. — A Gentleman of France.

WILKINS, M. E. — An Humble Romance.

—— Short Stories.

—— Pembroke.

XIV. SOME GOOD BOOKS AND STORIES THAT EVERY PERSON SHOULD KNOW.

FOUNDATION BOOKS.

ANDREWS, J. — Ten Boys on the Road from Long Ago
to Now.

BEESLY. — Stories from Rome.

BALDWIN. — The Story of Siegfried.

BIBLE, The. — Its stories; its character; its poetry.

BRYANT, W. C. (Trans.) — The Iliad.

—— The Odyssey.

BULFINCH, T. — Age of Fable.

—— Age of Chivalry.

—— Tales of Charlemagne.

BUNYAN, J. — Pilgrim's Progress.

CERVANTES. — Don Quixote.

CLOUGH, A. H. (Trans.) — Plutarch's Lives.

FISKE, J. — History of the United States.

FROST, W. H. — The Wagner Story Book.

GREENE, W. — History of England.

KINGSLEY, C. — The Greek Heroes.

MABIE, H. W. — Norse Stories.

MALORY. — Morte d'Arthur.

RAGOZIN. — Stories of Chaldea.

Shakespeare's Dramas.

BOOKS OF UNUSUAL INTEREST.

BARRIE, J. — Margaret Ogilvie.

BURROUGHS, J. — Pepacton.

CURTIS, G. W. — Prue and I.

JACKSON, H. H. — Bits of Travel at Home.
LAMB, C. — Essay of Elia.
MITCHELL, D. G. (Ik Marvel). — Reveries of a Bachelor.
—— About Old Story-tellers.
ROGER DE COVERLEY. — Papers from the Spectator.
THOREAU, H. D. — Walden.
WARNER, C. D. — My Summer in a Garden.

SHORT STORIES.

ANDERSEN, HANS. — The Ugly Duckling.
ALDRICH, T. B. — Marjorie Daw.
BROWN, DR. J. — Rab and his Friends.
DE LA RAME (Ouida). — The Dog of Flanders.
DICKENS, C. — A Christmas Carol.
HALE, E. E. — A Man without a Country.
HARTE, B. — Luck of Roaring Camp.
HAWTHORNE, N. — The Great Stone Face.
IRVING, W. — Rip Van Winkle.
JEWETT, S. O. — The White Heron.
KIPLING, R. — The Brush-wood Boy.
LAMB, C. — Dream-children.
LESSING. — Nathan the Wise.
POE, E. A. — The Gold-bug.
RUSKIN, J. — The King of the Golden River.
WARNER, C. D. — The Hunting of the Deer.
WILKINS, M. E. — A New England Nun.
—— The Revolt of Mother.

XV. REFERENCES UPON THE STUDY OF FICTION.

History of Fiction.

DUNLOP, J. C. — History of Prose Fiction (to 1814). 2 vols. 1888.

JUSSERAND, J. J. — English Novel in the time of Shakespeare. 1890.

MASSON, D. — British Novelists and their Styles. 1849.

RALEIGH, W. A. — English Novel: its History to the Appearance of Waverley. 1894.

RICHARDSON, C. F. — American Poetry and Fiction. (In his American Literature.) 1889.

SCOTT, SIR W. — Lives of Eminent Novelists and Dramatists.

TUCKERMAN, B. — History of English Prose Fiction.

Art of Fiction.

How to Write Fiction. Anon. Bellair & Co., London. 1895. Practical.

BESANT, W. — Art of Fiction. 1884.

BULWER-LYTTON, E. G. E. L. — Art in Fiction. (In his pamphlets and sketches.) 1875.

CRAWFORD, F. M. — The Novel: What It Is.

FREYTAG. The Technique of the Drama. (Trans.)

JAMES, H., Jr. — Art of Fiction. (In his Partial Portraits.) 1888.

KIPLING, R. — Life's Handicap. 1891. (Preface.) A Hindu tells Kipling the art of story-telling.

LANIER, S. — English Novel and the Principle of its Development.

MATTHEWS, B. — Art and Mystery of Collaboration. (In his With my Friends.) 1891.

—— Dramatization of Novels. (In his Studies of the Stage. 1894. Pp. 1–38.)

—— Philosophy of the Short Story. (In his Pen and Ink. 1888. Pp. 67–94.)

SMITH, G. — Lamps of Fiction. (In his Lectures and Essays. 1888. Pp. 75–96.)

THOMPSON, D. G. — Philosophy of Fiction in Literature.

ESSAYS ON FICTION.

BOYESON, H. H. — Literary and Social Silhouettes. 1894.

BRIDGES, R. (Droch). — Overheard in Arcady. 1894.

—— Suppressed Chapters and Other Bookishness. 1895.

GARLAND, H. — Crumbling Idols. "The genuine American literature must come from the soil and open air and be freed from tradition."

GOSSE, E. W. — Tyranny of the Novel. Limits of Realism in Fiction. (In his Questions at Issue. 1893. Pp. 1–31; 135–154.)

GREG, W. E. — False Morality of Lady Novelists. French Fiction : the Lowest Deep. (In his Literary and Social Judgments. 1876. Pp. 85–114; 146–181.)

HAWTHORNE, J. — Confessions and Criticisms. 1887.

HOWELLS, W. D. — Criticism and Fiction. 1891. Harper's.

JAMES, W. P. — Romantic Professions and Other Papers. 1894.

JEROME, J. K. (ed.). — My First Book. 1894. Contributions by twenty-two authors.

Library Journal. 1891. Addresses upon fiction in libraries.

MATTHEWS, B. — Story of a Story. 1893. On the influence of fiction.

NORDAU, M. — Degeneration. 1895.

PAGET, V. — On Novels. (In her Baldwin. 1886. Pp. 185-245.)

PHILIPSON, D. — The Jew in English Fiction. 1889. Jew of Malta, Merchant of Venice, Cumberland's The Jew, Ivanhoe, Oliver Twist, Our Mutual Friend, Coningsby, Tancred, Daniel Deronda.

RUSKIN, J. — Fiction, Fair and Foul. (In his Miscellanies.)

SAINTSBURY, G. E. B. — Present State of the English Novel. (In his Miscellaneous Essays. 1892. Pp. 388-426.)

SCOTT, SIR W. — Essays on Romance. (In his Chivalry, etc. 1870. Pp. 127-216.)

STEARNS, F. P. — Romance, Humor, and Realism; Modern Novel. (In his Real and Ideal in Literature. 1892. Pp. 10-76.)

STEVENSON, R. L. — Gossip on a Novel of Dumas'. Gossip on Romance. Humble Remonstrance. (In his Memories and Portraits. 1887. Pp. 228-299.)

TOWNSEND, M. E. (ed.). — Great Characters of Fiction. 1893.

TROLLOPE, A. — Autobiography. Chap. XII.

WHIPPLE, E. P. — Novels and Novelists. (In his Literature and Life. 1888. Pp. 42-83.)

CRITICISM BY AUTHORS AND SOME LESS IMPORTANT ESSAYS.

BROWNSON, O. A. — Religious Novels: Novel Writing and Novel Reading.

CRAIK, MRS. D. M. M. — On Novels and Novel-makers. (In her Plain-speaking. 1882. Pp. 118–143.)

ELIOT, G. (Evans.) — Essays and Leaves from a Note Book.

HAZELTINE, M. W. — Chats about Books, Poets, and Novelists. 1883.

HENLEY, W. E. — Views and Reviews. 1890.

HOWELLS, W. D. — My Literary Passions.

JAMES, H. — Partial Portraits. 1888.

LANG, A. — Essays in Little. 1891.

—— Old Friends. 1890. Imaginary letters of heroes and heroines in fiction.

MATTHEWS, B. — Americanisms and Briticisms. 1892.

MOORE, G. — Impressions and Opinions. 1891.

REPPLIER, A. — Essays in Miniature. 1892.

—— Points of View. 1891.

SCOTT, SIR W. — Criticism on Novels and Romances. (In his Periodical Criticism. 1870. Vols. II and III.)

STEPHEN, L. — Hours in a Library. 3 vols. 1874–1879.

HISTORICAL NOVELS.

ALISON, SIR A. — Historical Romance. (In his Essays. 1850. Pp. 521–559.)

ALLEN, W. F. — Historical Fiction. (In his Essays and Monographs. 1890. Pp. 112–128.)

CHOATE, R. — Importance of Illustrating New England by a Series of Romances like the Waverley Novels.

CLASSIFIED LIST FOR ENGLISH PROSE FICTION.

Boston Public Library. Chronological Index to Historical Fiction.

BOWEN, H. C. — Descriptive Catalogue of Historical Novels and Tales. 1882.

DIXON, Z. A. — Bibliography of Fiction.

GRISWOLD, W. M. — Descriptive Lists of Novels and Tales.

—— American City Life. 1891.

—— American Country Life. 1890.

—— Ancient History. 1895.

—— British Novels. 1891.

—— History of North America. 1895.

—— International Novels. 1891.

—— Life in France. 1892.

—— Life in Italy. 1892.

—— Life in Russia. 1892.

—— Romantic Novels. 1890.

Literary World. 1881. Vol. XII, pp. 57–60.

Los Angeles Public Library. List of Novels. Classified.

San Francisco Free Public Library. Classified English Prose Fiction. 1891. Said to be "the best-arranged fiction catalogue ever made."

MAGAZINE ARTICLES UPON FICTION.

ALLEN, J. L. — Two Principles of Recent Fiction. *Atlantic*, Oct. 1897, p. 133.

BESANT, W. — The Art of Fiction. *Critic*. 1: 297.

BOURGET, P. — The Limits of Realism in Fiction. *New Review*, Vol. VIII.

—— The Dangers of the Analytic Spirit in Fiction. *New Review*. Vol. VI.

CABLE, G. W. — After-thoughts of a Story-teller. *Nor. Am.*, Vol. CLVIII.

FORD, P. L. — The American Historical Novel. *Atlantic*, Dec. 1897, p. 721.

How to Write Short Stories. *Writer*, 2: 247.

How not to Write Fiction. *Lippincott's*, 40.

How to Write a Story. *Writer*, 2: 239.

LANG, A. — The Art of Fiction. *Critic*, 4: 249.

MATTHEWS, B. — The Philosophy of the Short Story. *Lippincott's*, October, 1885. *Sat. Rev.*, Vol. LVIII, p. 32, July, 1884.

PAGET, V. (Vernon Lee). — On Literary Construction. *Bookman*, N. Y., Vol. II, Nos. 1 and 2.

PERRY, B. — The Study of Fiction in College. *Mod. Lang. Assoc.*, Transactions XI. I.

STEVENSON, R. L. — The Art of Fiction. *Critic*, 5: 264.

Short Stories and their Writing. *Writer*, 5: 211.

TRAIL. — Romanticism Realisticised. *Contemp.*, 59.

The Deceitful Short Story. *Writer*, 2: 287.

THE STUDY OF FICTION.

MOULTON, R. G. (ed.). — Four Years of Novel Reading. The work of a club in a mining village in England.

SIMONDS, W. E. — Introduction to the Study of English Fiction.

DICTIONARIES FOR REFERENCE.

Century Dictionary of names.

BREWER, E. C. — Reader's Handbook of Allusions, References, Plots, and Stories. 1888.

WHEELER, W. A. Explanatory and Pronouncing Dictionary of the Noted Names of Fiction. 1889.

Best Novels.

Jones, J. L. (ed.). — Ten Great Novels. (In *Unity Club Leaflets*, 1891. p. 23.) These novels were chosen by the votes of seventy literary persons. The titles are: Scarlet Letter, Les Misérables, Romola, Adam Bede, Ivanhoe, Henry Esmond, Wilhelm Meister, Uncle Tom's Cabin, On the Heights, David Copperfield.

Perkins, F. B. — Best Hundred Novels. (*Library Journal*, 1876, Vol. VI. pp. 166, 167.)

INDEX.

ADVERTISEMENTS

English Composition and Rhetoric

Text-books and works of reference for
high schools, academies, and colleges.

Lessons in English. Adapted to the study of American Classics. A text-book for high schools and academies. By SARA E. H. LOCK-WOOD, formerly Teacher of English in the High School, New Haven Conn. Cloth. 403 pages. For introduction, $1.12.

A Practical Course in English Composition. By ALPHONSO G. NEW-COMER, Assistant Professor of English in Leland Stanford Junior University. Cloth. 249 pages. For introduction, 80 cents.

A Method of English Composition. By T. WHITING BANCROFT, late Professor of Rhetoric and English Literature in Brown University. Cloth. 101 pages. For introduction, 50 cents.

The Practical Elements of Rhetoric. By JOHN F. GENUNG, Professor of Rhetoric in Amherst College. Cloth. 483 pages. For introduction, $1.25.

A Handbook of Rhetorical Analysis. Studies in style and invention, designed to accompany the author's *Practical Elements of Rhetoric*. By JOHN F. GENUNG. Cloth. 306 pages. Introduction and teachers' price, $1.12.

Outlines of Rhetoric. Embodied in rules, illustrative examples, and a progressive course of prose composition. By JOHN F. GENUNG. Cloth. 331 pages. For introduction, $1.00.

The Principles of Argumentation. By GEORGE P. BAKER, Assistant Professor of English in Harvard University. Cloth. 414 pages. For introduction, $1.12.

The Forms of Discourse. With an introductory chapter on style. By WILLIAM B. CAIRNS, Instructor in Rhetoric in the University of Wisconsin. Cloth. 356 pages. For introduction, $1.15.

Outlines of the Art of Expression. By J. H. GILMORE, Professor of Logic, Rhetoric, and English in the University of Rochester, N.Y. Cloth. 117 pages. For introduction, 60 cents.

The Rhetoric Tablet. By F. N. SCOTT, Assistant Professor of Rhetoric, University of Michigan, and J. V. DENNEY, Associate Professor of Rhetoric, Ohio State University. **No. 1**, white paper (ruled). **No. 2**, tinted paper (ruled). Sixty sheets in each. For introduction, 15 cents.

Public Speaking and Debate. A manual for advocates and agitators. By GEORGE JACOB HOLYOAKE. Cloth. 266 pages. For introduction, $1.00.

•

GINN & COMPANY, Publishers,

Boston. New York. Chicago. Atlanta. Dallas.

GAYLEY'S CLASSIC MYTHS

THE CLASSIC MYTHS IN ENGLISH LITERATURE.

Based chiefly on Bulfinch's "Age of Fable" (1855). Accompanied by an Interpretative and Illustrative Commentary.

EDITED BY

CHARLES MILLS GAYLEY,

Professor of the English Language and Literature in the University of California.

12mo. Half leather. 540 pages. Fully illustrated, together with 16 full-page illustrations. For introduction, $1.50.

ATTENTION is called to these special features of this book:

An introduction on the indebtedness of English poetry to the literature of fable; and on methods of teaching mythology.

An elementary account of myth-making and of the principal poets of mythology, and of the beginnings of the world, of gods and of men among the Greeks.

A thorough revision and systematization of Bulfinch's Stories of Gods and Heroes : with additional stories, and with selections from English poems based upon the myths.

Illustrative cuts from Baumeister, Roscher, and other standard authorities on mythology.

Certain necessary modifications in Bulfinch's treatment of the mythology of nations other than the Greek and Roman.

Notes, following the text (as in the school editions of Latin and Greek authors), containing an historical and interpretative commentary upon certain myths, supplementary poetical citations, a list of the better known allusions to mythological fiction, references to works of art, and hints to teachers and students.

———

GINN & COMPANY, Publishers,

Boston.   New York.   Chicago.   Atlanta.   Dallas.

Reference Books on Poetry

·

A Book of Elizabethan Lyrics. Selected and edited by Felix E. Schelling, Professor of English Literature in the University of Pennsylvania. 327 pages. For introduction, $1.12.

Old English Ballads. Selected and edited by Professor F. B. Gummere of Haverford College. 380 pages. For introduction, $1.25.

Introduction to the Poetry of Robert Browning. By William J. Alexander, Professor of English, University College, Toronto. 212 pages. For introduction, $1.00.

Hudson's Text-Book of Poetry. By Henry N. Hudson. Selections from Wordsworth, Coleridge, Burns, Beattie, Goldsmith, and Thomson. With Lives and Notes. Cloth. 704 pages. For introduction, $1.25.

Sidney's Defense of Poesy. Edited by Albert S. Cook, Professor of the English Language and Literature in Yale University. 103 pages. For introduction, 80 cents.

Shelley's Defense of Poetry. Edited by Professor Albert S. Cook. 86 pages. For introduction, 50 cents.

Cardinal Newman's Essay on Poetry. With reference to Aristotle's Poetics. Edited by Professor Albert S. Cook. 36 pages. For introduction, 30 cents.

The Art of Poetry. The Poetical Treatises of Horace, Vida, and Boileau, with the translations by Howes, Pitt, and Soame. Edited by Professor Albert S. Cook. 214 pages. For introduction, $1.12.

Addison's Criticisms on Paradise Lost. Edited by Professor Albert S. Cook. 200 pages. For introduction, $1.00.

What is Poetry? By Leigh Hunt. Edited by Professor Albert S. Cook. 98 pages. For introduction, 50 cents.

A Primer of English Verse. By Hiram Corson, Professor of English Literature in Cornell University. 232 pages. For introduction, $1.00.

A Hand-Book of Poetics. By Francis B. Gummere, Professor of English Literature in Haverford College. 75 pages. For introduction, $1.00.

Characteristics of the English Poets, from Chaucer to Shirley. By William Minto. For introduction, $1.50.

GINN & COMPANY, Publishers,

Boston.   **New York.**   **Chicago.**   **Atlanta.**   **Dallas**

STANDARD ENGLISH CLASSICS

EDITED BY COMPETENT SCHOLARS WITH SPECIAL REFERENCE TO COLLEGE REQUIREMENTS.

Tennyson's The Princess. Edited by ALBERT S. COOK, Professor of English Literature in Yale University. 40 cents.

Carlyle's Essay on Burns. Edited by CHARLES L. HANSON, Teacher of English in the Mechanic Arts High School, Boston, Mass. 30 cents.

Macaulay's Essay on Milton. Edited by HERBERT A. SMITH, Instructor in English in Yale University. 25 cents.

Macaulay's Essay on Addison. Edited by HERBERT A. SMITH. 35 cents.

Macaulay's Essays on Addison and Milton. (In one volume.) Edited by HERBERT A. SMITH. 50 cents.

Dryden's Palamon and Arcite. Edited by GEORGE E. ELIOT, Jr., Instructor in English in Morgan School, Clinton, Conn. 35 cents.

George Eliot's Silas Marner. Edited by R. ADELAIDE WITHAM, Teacher of English in Latin High School, Somerville, Mass. 50 cents.

Sir Roger de Coverley Papers. From "*The Spectator.*" Edited by MARY E. LITCHFIELD. cents.

Coleridge's Ancient Mariner. Edited by L. R. GIBBS. 25 cents.

Pope's Translation of the Iliad. *Books I., VI., XXII., and XXIV.* Edited by WILLIAM TAPPAN. 35 cents.

Macaulay's Lays of Ancient Rome. Edited by M. GRANT DANIELL, recently Principal of Chauncy-Hall School. cents.

Cooper's Last of the Mohicans. Edited by JOHN B. DUNBAR, Instructor in English in the Boys' High School, Brooklyn, N. Y. 60 cents.

Shakespeare's Macbeth. Edited by Rev. HENRY N. HUDSON. 35 cents.

Burke's Speech on Conciliation with America. Edited by HAMMOND LAMONT, Associate Professor of Rhetoric in Brown University. 40 cents.

Goldsmith's Vicar of Wakefield. Edited by D. H. MONTGOMERY. 4 cents.

Edmund Burke's Letter to a Noble Lord. Edited by ALBERT H. SMYTH, Professor of English Literature in the Central High School, Philadelphia. 30 cents.

Irving's Sketch Book. (Complete.) Edited, with Introduction and Notes, by MARY E. LITCHFIELD. cents.

De Quincey's Revolt of the Tartars. Edited by W. E. SIMONDS, Professor of English Literature in Knox College, Galesburg, Ill. 30 cents.

Milton's Paradise Lost, Books I. and II., and Lycidas. Edited by HOMER B. SPRAGUE.

—

GINN & COMPANY, Publishers,

Boston.   New York.   Chicago.   Atlanta.   Dallas.

www.ingramcontent.com/pod-product-compliance
Lightning Source LLC
Chambersburg PA
CBHW022343020726
47500CB00004B/1255